MW01129751

youth - 96

PAST AND PRESENT

DISCRIMINATION

ANGELA PHILLIPS

New York

First American publication 1993 by New Discovery Books, Macmillan Publishing Company, 866 Third Avenue, New York, NY 10022

Macmillan Publishing Company is part of the Maxwell Communication Group of Companies

First published in 1993 by Heinemann Library, an imprint of Heinemann Educational, a division of Heinemann Publishers (Oxford) Ltd, Halley Court, Jordan Hill, Oxford OX2 8EJ

Devised and produced by Zoë Books Limited
15 Worthy Lane, Winchester, SO23 7AB, England

Edited by Charlotte Rolfe
Picture research by Faith Perkins
Designed by Julian Holland

Printed in China

Library of Congress Cataloging-in-Publication Data

Phillips, Angela.
 Discrimination / Angela Phillips.
  p. cm. — (Past and present)
 Summary: Examines the history of discrimination and prejudice from its first recorded appearance in 380 a.d. to present crisis between different races, religions, and class systems.
 ISBN 0-02-786881-8
 1. Discrimination — History — Juvenile-literature. 2. Sex discrimination against women — History — Juvenile literature. 3. Race discrimination — History — Juvenile literature. [1. Discrimination — History. 2. Prejudices. 3. Minorities.] I. Title. II. Series.
 HM291.P487   1993
 305 — dc20
                                                    92-33946

Photographic acknowledgments

The author and publishers wish to acknowledge, with thanks, the following photographic sources: Sally and Richard Greenhill p 11: Hulton-Deutsch Collection pp 7; 12; 19; 37: IMPACT p 25: International Aid and Defence Fund p 33: Magnum pp 4 (Meiselas); 15, 34 (Abbas): Peter Newark's Western Americana p 29: Popperfoto pp 23; 39: Topham Picture Source pp title page; 9; 14; 31; 41.

The cover photograph is courtesy of Topham Picture Source.

Title page: This auto worker has been beaten up during a "Red" hunt. During the early 1950s, when anti-communist feelings ran high in the United States, anyone even suspected of being a communist could face similar treatment.

CONTENTS

EQUALITY FOR ALL ?

In 1989 as part of the Iraqi government's campaign against
the Kurds living in northern Iraq, Saddam Hussein ordered
the bombing of the Kurdish town of Qaladiza. These Kurdish
women are preparing traditional bread on the roof of their
home, which was destroyed during the bombing.

EQUALITY FOR ALL

In many different parts of the world today, people are struggling against unfair treatment, or **discrimination.** At the same time, there are individuals, political organizations, and even governments who argue that "foreigners should be sent home," or that people of a different race or religion should be "kept in their place." Some believe that it is perfectly acceptable for men and women to receive different pay for the same work, or that someone who objects to being treated differently is simply "a troublemaker."

A WORD AND ITS MEANING

In the seventeenth and eighteenth centuries to discriminate simply meant to notice differences. The word is still used to mean this today. People are sometimes described as "discriminating" in their choice of clothes. This means they choose their clothes carefully.

In the nineteenth century the word began to take on a different meaning. It was used to mean the ways in which black people were treated differently from white people. In 1899 the African-American leader Booker T. Washington used the words "unjust discrimination" to describe the effects of many laws and customs on African-Americans in the United States.

In British law today discrimination means any form of unequal treatment of people because of their sex, race, color, or nationality. American law includes unequal treatment on the grounds of religion. But these are not the only causes of discrimination. People are also discriminated against because of their **social classes.** Disabled people often face discrimination, along with other groups popularly labeled as "different," such as homosexuals.

When individuals experience discrimination they suffer in some way. Their lives are restricted. They do not enjoy the same opportunities as other people. They may be the victims of violence, especially if they try to change their situation. Most people would agree that this is unfair. So why do some groups discriminate against others?

HOLDING ON TO POWER

Discrimination is one way people can hold on to power and keep it for themselves. Governments sometimes discriminate against the people who oppose them.

In 1948 the Jewish state of Israel was founded. Its founding was strongly opposed by neighboring Arab states and by the Arabs living inside Israel itself. Since 1948 a number of wars have been fought between Israel and the Arab states. Some Arabs have used terrorism against Israeli rule. The government of Israel has discriminated against its Arab citizens because they are considered enemies. Most of the land in Israel is reserved for Jews. Thousands of Arabs have been imprisoned as a punishment for opposing the government.

Sometimes governments discriminate against totally innocent people because they get in the way of sweeping changes. During the 1930s Joseph Stalin, the ruler of the former Soviet Union, seized the farmers' land. After that time, all farms were to be owned by the state. Millions of *kulaks* — independent peasant farmers — were sent to **concentration camps.** Millions more were deliberately starved to death. Stalin was determined to crush all opposition to his ideas about state control of agriculture.

For many centuries the Kurdish people have lived in an area of the Middle East known as Kurdistan. Today this area overlaps three different countries. Innocent Kurds have suffered because some of their leaders have demanded an independent Kurdish state. The governments of Iran, Iraq, and Turkey have all discriminated against their Kurdish citizens. In Turkey publications in the Kurdish language are banned; in Iraq many Kurdish villages have been destroyed and thousands of families forced to flee.

HOLDING ON TO PRIVILEGE

In almost all societies, some people have more wealth and **privilege** than others. Discrimination is an effective way of keeping up this kind of inequality. People who have wealth and privilege can discriminate against others to keep them in their place.

The schoolboys in the top photograph, taken in a poor part of London's East End in 1911, would have had little chance of finding well-paid jobs when they left school. On the other hand, the boys in the bottom photograph, taken at the exclusive private school of Eton, in England, would probably have had prosperous futures already planned.

For many hundreds of years Indian society was divided into **castes.** The higher castes were landowners, priests, and warriors. The lower castes were servants and laborers. It was impossible for a person to change his or her caste. If you were born into a certain caste you had to stay in it for life.

Many societies today are divided into social classes. It is possible for a person to change his or her social class but discrimination may make this difficult. Throughout the nineteenth century in Britain children whose parents were poor or working class had little or no education. As a result it was almost impossible for these children to change their position in society when they grew up. They were most likely to remain doing the same unskilled,˙low-paid work their parents had always done.

Although there is less class discrimination today than in the past, it has not completely disappeared. A person with a working-class accent may still find it more difficult to get a good job than someone with a middle- or upper-class accent. People who have important positions in society, such as judges, bankers, and leading government officials, are still mostly drawn from the upper and middle classes.

PREJUDICE

Prejudice is one of the most prevailing reasons why people discriminate against others. It means disliking people because of their sex, color, religion, age, or some other characteristic. Prejudiced people usually believe that they and others like them are better than people who are different in some way.

Prejudice is based on ignorance. It is not based on fact or reality. We can see this if we listen to what prejudiced people say. Prejudiced people in the United States, for example, sometimes accuse **immigrants** of "coming here to take our jobs." They also say that immigrants "don't come here to work, they come here to live off state benefits." It is obvious to any thinking person that both these statements cannot be true. So why do people go on being prejudiced?

It can be extremely difficult to persuade prejudiced

A popular English actress takes time off to support a petition against age discrimination in Britain. In the past older people were usually respected, but today even people in their fifties are being encouraged to retire and are often the first to lose their jobs.

people to change their minds, because they are so convinced they are right. Even people who are not prejudiced themselves are sometimes influenced by what prejudiced people think. A man who is not prejudiced against a woman may still refuse to give a woman a job, because he fears that the other men he works with will be angry and criticize him.

> "The truth is that at first color doesn't mean very much to little children, black or white. Only as they grow older and absorb poisons from adults does color begin to blind them."
>
> *Roy Wilkins, American writer, 1982*

Some religious and racial groups are very proud of their traditions. They prefer to live in their own communities, where they can keep their beliefs and customs alive. This sometimes encourages prejudice from others. It is easy for us to become suspicious of people when we do not know them well. It is also easy to develop false and ignorant ideas about them. Yet people who are discriminated against are often unable to mix freely with others. Disabled people, for example, may find it difficult to get work in offices, factories, or stores where they can meet and get to know others. It may be impossible for them to use movie theaters, restaurants, swimming pools, and other places. Most able-bodied people never meet any disabled people or have much contact with them. They may assume that someone in a wheelchair is probably a bit stupid. So prejudice and discrimination are both closely linked. This is what makes discrimination such a lasting problem and such a difficult one to solve.

A MODERN PROBLEM?

Today's use and meaning of the word "discrimination" might make one think that it is a problem belonging to the last hundred years or so. However, if we look further back into the past, we can see that this is not true.

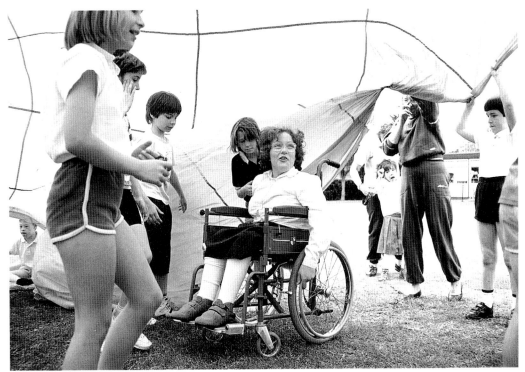

Some disabled children attend ordinary schools, either by choice or because there are no suitable special schools. If the school is welcoming, it can be a good opportunity for the children to mix and get to know one another better.

Many of the world's earliest civilizations depended on the work of conquered peoples for their basic needs. About 2,600 years ago in Sparta, a state in ancient Greece, the defeated inhabitants, known as helots, had to grow all the food required by their masters, and support them in times of war. As members of a slave class, neither the helots nor their children could share in the freedoms and privileges enjoyed by Spartan citizens. Instead they were despised and badly treated. Prejudice and discrimination were as common in the ancient world as they are today.

"No man is good enough to be another man's master."

George Bernard Shaw, Irish writer, 1905

A WOMAN'S PLACE ?

Early in the twentieth century it was still the custom in China for upper-class women to have their feet bound as a sign of their dependence. The injury caused to their feet restricted their movements and their freedom.

Have women always been discriminated against? Are women equal to men in the world today? Questions like these often cause fierce arguments and debates. They are difficult to answer unless we look at women's lives at different times and in different places.

HUNTERS AND GATHERERS

When people first appeared on the earth, and for thousands of years afterward, they lived as hunters and gatherers. They lived in small tribes and moved from place to place, hunting animals and gathering plants for food. They spent much of their time and energy finding and carrying water and fuel. Other important tasks were building shelters and looking after young children.

Women in hunting and gathering societies were treated with respect. The work they did was essential for the survival of the tribe. The women of the San people of South Africa were responsible for lighting and taking care of fires. Without fires the San would not have been able to cook their food, keep warm at night, or frighten away dangerous animals.

In some hunting and gathering tribes, women and men shared all the important tasks equally. Women and men of the Mbuti people in Central Africa took an equal part in hunting, gathering, and looking after children. Women sometimes had a great deal of authority, too. The Hopi of North America elected women as their leaders.

> "If woman had not been created, there would have been no sun and no moon, no agriculture and no fire."
>
> *Arab saying*

RELIGION

Prejudice against women sometimes comes from religion. In the ancient Chinese religion Confucianism, women were thought of as stupid, timid, and ignorant. These views were widely held for over 2,000 years. Chinese women were treated as the property of their male relatives.

Three people being hanged as witches in England in 1589. Women became afraid of appearing too knowledgable in case they were accused of being witches.

As children, girls had far fewer opportunities and faced harsher punishments than the boys in the family. Their lives were ruled by the Three Obediences: unmarried girls had to obey their fathers and brothers; married women had to obey their husbands; widows had to obey their adult sons.

In the early Christian Church, too, men were instructed by their priests to control the female members of their families. The early Christian Church was determined to stamp out **pagan** beliefs and rituals. Women who practiced traditional ways of healing were sometimes accused of being witches and were publicly executed.

"Women should learn in silence and all humility. I do not allow them to teach or have authority over men. They must keep quiet."

From Paul's Epistle to Timothy in the
New Testament of the Bible

THE LAW

The religion of a country influences its laws. The law in some Islamic countries, such as Iran and Saudi Arabia, insists that women wear veils in public. For hundreds of years British laws discriminated against women. When a woman married, all her money and possessions became the property of her husband. Until 1878 a wife had no right in law to leave her husband even if he was violent to her. By the end of the nineteenth century most men in Britain had the right to vote. Women had no political rights at all.

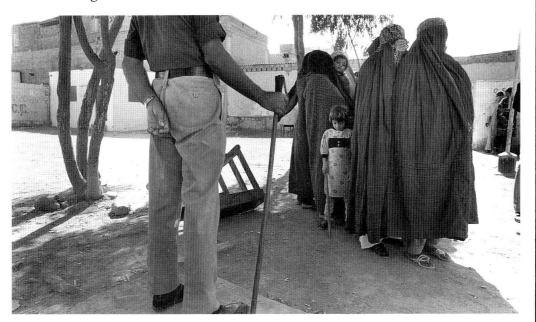

In Pakistan, as in many Islamic countries, women must still wear a veil in public. This veil hides them from men or strangers who may see them.

WORK

Women everywhere have a long history of work. In Europe women worked alongside men in the fields for hundreds of years. They also worked in craft industries such as spinning and weaving cloth. After the **industrial revolution,** however, ideas about women and work changed, especially among the members of the new, wealthy classes. Having a job came to be seen as something only men should do. Husbands should be the "breadwinners." They should earn money to provide for their families. Women should stay at home. Their job was to be housewives looking after the home and the children. Middle-class women and girls were not allowed to work. However, many working-class women had to work in order to survive in the new industrial cities that grew up at this time. Their families needed the money they could earn. They were paid much less than men, often for work that was just as hard. Many young women and girls went to work as servants for wealthy families.

> "Women are nothing but machines for producing children."
>
> *Napoleon Bonaparte,*
> *French Emperor 1804-1815*

In the mid-twentieth century women gradually gained more job opportunities. They could now become office workers, nurses, or teachers. A few managed to become doctors or lawyers. Sex discrimination continued, however. A woman was paid much less than a man doing exactly the same job. In Britain almost all jobs had a "marriage bar." This meant that women were forced to leave work when they got married. Janet Young was one of the first women to work in the Bank of England. After her wedding she kept her marriage a secret for four years because she did not want to lose her job. Obvious discrimination like this lasted a long time. The marriage bar stayed in place until World War II.

BELLA KEYSER

During World War II (1939-1945), the lives of British and American women were turned upside down. Men were sent away to fight. Women were expected to do many of the jobs the men had left behind. The government opened nurseries for young children, so that their mothers could work.

The war gave many women their first chance to earn a good wage and gain some independence. Some had the opportunity to learn new skills and do interesting work. One such woman was Bella Keyser. She was sent to work in a shipbuilding yard near her home in Scotland. She was taught how to be a welder. She learned how to join pieces of metal with special tools. Bella enjoyed her new job very much and she liked working in the busy shipyard. When the war was over, Bella had to leave. The men were coming back home and returning to the jobs they had left. Many women lost their jobs at the end of the war. The nurseries closed and women were expected to go back to being housewives. Bella Keyser tried many times to get another job as a welder. Every time she tried, she was told that welding was a man's job. None of the shipyards would give her the job she wanted because she was a woman. In 1975 the British government passed the Sex Discrimination Act. This meant that it was now against the law to refuse to give someone a job because of his or her sex. Bella Keyser went down to the shipyard and asked for a job as a welder. This time the managers could not say no without breaking the law. Bella became a welder again after 30 years of waiting and trying.

EDUCATION

Throughout the first half of this century and beyond, sex discrimination affected the lives of children at school, both in Europe and the United States. Girls and boys were taught different subjects. Boys learned skills that would be useful at work. Girls were taught cooking, dressmaking, and how to look after children. The idea was that girls should learn how to be good housewives.

Prejudice also helped to keep women out of public life. In the nineteenth century women were thought to be less intelligent than men because they had smaller brains. Educating girls, it was said, would damage their health. Some people believed it might make them unable to have babies!

WOMEN TODAY

How are the lives of women different today? Sex discrimination is against the law in many countries, such as China, Russia, the United States, and most European countries. However, this does not mean that it has disappeared. Women are still discriminated against at work. Some men still believe that women are not capable of doing a responsible or difficult job. All over the world, most women earn less than men. All over the world, the jobs with low pay are thought of as women's work. Women pick tea in Sri Lanka. They are domestic servants in South America. In richer countries they work in offices, answering the telephone and typing. Women can get jobs like these because men do not want them.

Some countries have had women prime ministers. Throughout the world, however, most politicians are men. Many people still believe that the home is women's special responsibility. It is difficult for women to find enough time to care for their families *and* have responsible jobs. Many women have to take part-time work and so they can only earn low wages. Most single parents are women. They have to look after their children on their own and try to earn enough money to support them.

Governments in the poorer countries of the world often cannot afford to provide schools for all children. In some countries twice as many boys as girls go to school. Parents still think that educating boys is more important than educating girls. There are many more women than men in the world today who cannot read or write.

FREEDOM OF BELIEF?

This sixteenth-century bookseller is being burned for selling
Bibles in his shop at Avignon, in France. The offending
Bibles can be seen hung around his neck. He was a Protestant
being burned by Catholics. Catholics in countries with
Protestant rulers suffered similar fates.

Throughout history people have experienced discrimination because of their religious beliefs. Sometimes certain religious beliefs have been seen as a threat by governments or powerful people, leading to all-out **persecution.**

THE MEDIEVAL CHURCH

In the Middle Ages (around A.D. 800-1500) the Roman Catholic Church in Europe had great power and wealth. Church leaders were suspicious of any religious beliefs and ideas that did not come from the Church itself. Christian beliefs that were not approved of by the Church were condemned as heresy, or false beliefs. During the eleventh century the Cathar heresy spread very quickly. The Cathars believed that Jesus Christ was a spirit, rather than a real person. This belief was contrary to the teachings of the Roman Catholic Church. Many people in the southern part of France became Cathars. They no longer listened to the Catholic priests and they stopped paying taxes to the Church. Pope Innocent III was determined to destroy this threat to the Church's power. He declared a **crusade** against the Cathar heresy. Thousands of Cathars were massacred in a brutal war, and their property was taken by the crusaders and the Church itself. Eventually, after a hundred years of persecution, the Cathar heresy was totally wiped out.

RELIGION AND POLITICS

Europe was torn apart by religious wars during the sixteenth and seventeenth centuries. Catholics and Protestants fought against each other. Religion and politics were very closely connected at that time. Religion was not seen as a matter of individual freedom as it is today. The rulers of countries expected their subjects to have the same religion as they had themselves. Roman Catholic rulers did not trust any of their subjects who were Protestants. They feared their Protestant subjects might rebel in favor of a Protestant ruler. Protestants living in a country ruled by a Catholic were often accused of treason and punished by death. Protestant rulers were equally suspicious of Catholic subjects. Catholics risked imprisonment, torture, or death if they held on to their beliefs in a country ruled by a Protestant.

The way a ruler behaved often depended on the strength of his or her own religious beliefs. Queen Mary Tudor of England (1516-1558) was a devout Catholic. She believed that God wanted her to destroy Protestantism. During her five-year reign, 300 English Protestants were burned at the stake. The Protestant Queen Elizabeth I, who ruled immediately after Mary, was more concerned about politics than religion. She only punished Catholics when she believed they were plotting against her.

Religious discrimination and persecution did not only occur in Europe. Christian missionaries brought their faith to Japan in the sixteenth century. The powerful rulers there feared the spread of Christianity. They thought the new, foreign ideas would encourage the peasants to rebel. Many missionaries and Japanese Christians were tortured, beheaded, or burned to death.

DISCRIMINATION IN IRELAND

For many centuries Ireland was ruled by the kings and queens of England. Religion became a source of political conflict during the time of the religious wars. England became a Protestant country under Elizabeth I but Ireland was Roman Catholic. In 1688 King James II of England was forced from his throne because he was a Catholic. He tried to regain the throne by raising an army in Ireland but he was defeated. The English government punished the Irish with laws that discriminated against Catholics. These Penal Laws, as they were called, prevented Catholics from joining the army and the navy or becoming members of Parliament. English governments also gave Irish land to English and Scottish Protestants. Most Protestants settled in the north of the country.

Ireland became an independent country in 1922. However the Protestants in the north did not want to live in a Catholic country and the British government allowed six northern counties to remain a part of the United Kingdom. Most of the people in these six counties were

Protestant but about a third were Catholic. The Protestants in Northern Ireland controlled the government, most of the businesses, and the police. Catholics were discriminated against from the start. They were often refused jobs and houses. Protests against discrimination led to violent battles between demonstrators and the police. By the beginning of the 1970s Northern Ireland had almost reached a state of civil war. The British army was sent in to control the situation, but terrorist groups, both Catholic and Protestant, are still fighting today.

IDEAS AT WAR

As you have seen already in this chapter, religious discrimination and persecution are often closely linked with a struggle for power and influence. Sometimes people are discriminated against because their political ideas do not fit in with those of the government of the day. In 1973 the publicly elected **socialist** government of Chile was overthrown, and the army seized power. During the years that followed, anyone suspected of being a socialist or of having supported the socialist government was imprisoned. Many were tortured and executed.

In some countries those who are not members of the national political party may find they are discriminated against. In many of the former **communist** countries of eastern Europe, people who were not Communist party members were treated with suspicion. They found themselves passed over for promotion, housing, or educational opportunities. Many were spied upon by secret police. When the East German government fell in 1990 one of the first acts of the people was to destroy the building that contained secret files of information on thousands of ordinary citizens.

Political discrimination is common in states where no opposition is allowed, but it can happen in **democratic** countries, too. In the United States during the 1950s Senator Joseph McCarthy led a campaign to root out supposed Communists. Anyone who sympathized with communist ideas or who had communist friends was

These farmers and their families are being expelled from their village in Russia. It is 1930 and independent farmers are being forced off the land in order to make way for large state-run collective farms.

under suspicion. They were questioned, expelled from political life, or lost their jobs.

MINORITIES

Many religious **minorities** have suffered discrimination that has had nothing to do with politics or political opposition. From the eighth and ninth centuries in the early Islamic world non-Muslims were discriminated against. They had to pay special taxes and were not allowed to carry weapons. Jews and Christians living in the Muslim cities of the Middle East had to wear special clothing to distinguish them from the Muslims, and they could not defend themselves against a Muslim in a court of law.

In medieval Europe Jewish communities suffered centuries of discrimination and persecution. The

Christian Churches blamed them for the death of Jesus Christ. The first laws discriminating against Jews were passed when Christianity became the official religion of the Roman Empire. Whole Jewish communities were slaughtered at the end of the eleventh century during the first crusade — a time of extreme religious fervor.

The Jewish faith includes rules and regulations about everyday life. There are special rules about food and how it should be prepared, and about family life in general. The only way the Jews could preserve their religion and their traditions was by living in their own communities. For their part the Christian Churches would not allow their members to mix closely with Jews. Gradually, many strange lies and prejudices about the Jews became part of public opinion. Christians believed that Jews practiced witchcraft and worshiped the devil. When a plague known as the Black Death killed hundreds of thousands in the fourteenth century, rumors spread that Jews were poisoning the wells. When children were lost or kidnapped, Jews were accused of murdering them and using their blood in religious rituals.

Under laws that discriminated against them, Jews could not own land or work in most trades and professions. Some Jews turned to banking and lending money as a way of earning a living. Another prejudice was born as a result. All Jews, it was said, are naturally mean and greedy.

Even today, discrimination against religious minorities continues. Muslims of Turkish descent were persecuted in Bulgaria in the 1980s. The Bulgarian government wanted all its citizens to be the same. They were all to be Communists and speak the Bulgarian language. Minorities were no longer to be tolerated. Muslim women were forbidden to wear veils, mosques were closed, and Turks were forced to take Bulgarian names. When these methods did not work, the Muslims were expelled from their homes and their country.

RACE

An Australian Aboriginal family relaxes in the shade. After 150 years of persecution and discrimination by Europeans, Aboriginal peoples now have the vote and the right to state benefits, but must still struggle to preserve their language and culture within Australian society.

Race discrimination has a long history. Some ethnic groups have suffered from discrimination for hundreds of years. The Romany people — known as gypsies — first moved from Asia into Europe in the Middle Ages. They were darker in color than most Europeans. The way they dressed and the language they spoke seemed strange and unfamiliar to most people in Europe. Their nomadic way of life made many people suspicious of them. Governments suspected them of being criminals and the Church suspected them of witchcraft. They were often imprisoned and sold as slaves. Gypsy children were taken from their parents and brought up in peasant families. In the 1930s the **Nazis** tried to exterminate all gypsies in the same way they tried to exterminate all Jews in Germany and the countries they occupied during World War II. Notices saying "No gypsies or travelers" can be seen in Britain even today. This shows us how long race prejudice can last when it becomes fixed in people's minds.

Race discrimination can be used by one nation or people to control others, in much the same way as a class or caste system. During the seventeenth century, a people called the Tutsi moved southward from the Upper Nile to an area that today forms the Central African countries of Rwanda and Burundi. They forced the local people, the Hutu, to be their servants and do all the hard work. According to the Tutsi, the local people were strong but not very intelligent. In other words the Tutsi thought of themselves as a superior race. Although the Tutsi formed less than 20 percent of the population, they ruled over the Hutu for over 400 years.

CONQUEST AND EMPIRE

Most of the race discrimination in the world today is practiced by white people against people of other races. This situation is the result of 400 years of European control over much of the rest of the world. European explorers first claimed land in Central America in the fifteenth century. **Colonies** were established throughout the American continent. By 1914 European nations controlled four-fifths of the world's land surface. The native peoples of Australia, Asia, and Africa were conquered. Their land was seized. Millions were forced into slavery.

THE AMERICAS

The European colonists excused and defended their conquest of Native Americans with racial prejudice. In the eyes of the colonists the native peoples of the Americas were savages. Conquering and seizing their land was right because it was a holy cause, bringing Christianity to ignorant heathens.

The colonists also argued that it did not matter if Native Americans were slaughtered or forced to become slaves — they did not possess souls so they were not really human beings. However, the real reason for the conquest of the Americas was the search for wealth. The explorers and colonists were trying to find new trading routes, and they were hoping to discover gold.

> "I and my companions suffer from a disease of the heart which can only be cured with gold."
>
> *Hernando Cortes, conqueror of Mexico (1485-1547)*

SLAVERY

Vast numbers of slaves were used in the American colonies. The settlers could make fortunes from mining gold or growing sugar, cotton, and tobacco, but they needed workers. Native Americans were used as slaves, but too many died as a result of cruelty and disease. The shortage of labor was solved by importing slaves from Africa. The slave trade continued for 300 years.

Europeans argued that black people were suited to be slaves. According to white men, black people needed to be told what to do because they were not capable of thinking for themselves. They were naturally lazy so they would only work if forced to do so. Beliefs like these laid the foundations of the racial prejudice and discrimination that have lasted until today.

AUSTRALIA

The conquest of Australia involved 150 years of conflict between white settlers and the Aboriginals who had lived in Australia for thousands of years. Pat Dodson, an Aboriginal leader, explains what happened in these words:

"When the whites first came here they used the Latin phrase *terra nullius* to describe the land. That meant it was empty, unused. They knocked down the trees and blasted the sacred places. They fenced off the best water for their cattle. When we resisted, they shot and poisoned us."

Once the settlers had defeated the Aboriginals they had to find ways of controlling them. Many Aboriginals were forced to live in reservations. They could not leave the reservations without permission. They were forbidden to own dogs or weapons. In other words they lost all their freedom. Many native peoples in North America suffered the same treatment. They, too, were forced onto reservations.

SEGREGATION

In Australia some Aboriginals were needed by the colonists to work as servants and laborers. They were allowed to live near white people but they were **segregated**. This is a form of race discrimination that involves keeping people of different races apart. Aboriginals who lived in towns had to live in special areas that kept them separated from the whites. They were not allowed to use hotels, restaurants, or swimming pools. Rows of seats in movie theaters were roped off for Aboriginals to sit in. In the opinion of many white Australians, the Aboriginals were too primitive to be allowed to mix with whites.

Segregation was introduced in the southern United States after slavery was abolished at the end of the Civil War. Southern whites were determined to keep the freed slaves in their place. Laws were passed that segregated schools, hospitals, buses, and even blood banks. By 1900 almost every aspect of life was segregated by these "Jim Crow" laws, as they were called.

Segregation laws lasted for many years in parts of the United
States. This photograph, taken in 1945, shows a store in
Florida that was for black people only.

SHARECROPPING

In the southern United States, white landowners allowed
the freed slaves to farm portions of their land, but the
sharecroppers had to buy all their tools, clothes, and food
from the landowners on credit. They were supposed to
pay off their debts when they had harvested and sold their
crops. In fact the sharecroppers never made enough
money to repay their debts. They always owed the
landowners money. Most African-Americans in the
southern states were as poor and tied to the land as when
they were slaves. For many freedom was an illusion.

RIGHTS AND LIBERTIES

As well as abolishing slavery, the United States
government had granted citizenship to African-
Americans and had given them the right to vote.
Gradually, however, with the help of a whole range of
discrimination laws, the southern states took away this
right to vote. In the years following the Civil War a

violent, **racist** organization called the Ku Klux Klan terrorized and even murdered African-Americans who tried to exercise their rights or object to the way they were treated. Some moved to the North in search of a better life. They had to face discrimination, poverty, and racist violence in city **ghettos.**

FANTASY AND FACT

In the nineteenth century, new theories about superior and inferior races were developed by European scientists. Skulls of people of different races were collected and compared. The scientists concluded that the European skull was the only one that could contain a brain capable of logical thought. They argued that other races possessed inferior brains and needed the civilizing influence of Europeans to lift them out of primitive ignorance. However, these theories were based on racist assumptions and were only too clearly contradicted by the facts. For example, when British colonists arrived in India they came across one of the oldest and most advanced civilizations in the world. The sacred books of the Hindu religion, the Vedas, were written 2,000 years before the birth of Christ. Indians lived in large cities long before the ancient Greeks and Romans did. Indians built large sailing ships thousands of years before Europeans learned how to build them. The decimal number system, which is used throughout the world today, was invented in India.

JEWS IN NAZI GERMANY

During World War I (1914-1918), over 12,000 German Jews died fighting for their country. However, when Adolf Hitler and the Nazi party came to power in Germany in 1933, they claimed that all Jews were evil by nature and that they destroyed everything they came into contact with. Hitler immediately introduced laws to prevent Jews from working in government service. Two years later all German Jews were stripped of their German citizenship. The Nazis put their racist beliefs into practice and murdered six million Jews in a purge that shocked the world.

These Jewish people in Lublin, Poland, in 1941, are lining up to collect water. After the Nazis invaded Poland in 1939 they forced all Polish Jews to remain permanently within Jewish city ghettos. Many died from the results of overcrowding, lack of food, and regular attacks by armed Nazi troops.

RACE DISCRIMINATION TODAY

The history of conquest and empire can still be traced in the race discrimination found in the world today. In the Central American state of Guatemala the government kills and terrorizes people of native descent. Nearly 500 years after the Spanish conquest the native Americans are still seen as a threat to the state. Black people in the Americas and in Australia remain poorer than whites. They suffer more from poor health and disease and die at a younger age. Slavery and legal segregation have been outlawed, but equality has not been achieved.

People of Asian and African descent living in Europe often experience discrimination. They are sometimes blamed for many of the problems that affect European countries. In France and Britain racist political parties accuse Arab, African, and Asian groups of causing unemployment and other economic problems. In Germany, racist violence has broken out in recent years. The joining together of the two parts of Germany to form one nation has caused some Germans to feel uncertain about the future. Political groups with ideas similar to the Nazis' have appeared in this climate of uncertainty. Immigrants have been threatened, beaten up, and have had their homes destroyed.

History has given white people both power and privilege in many parts of the world, but it would be wrong to suppose that only white people discriminate on grounds of race.

Idi Amin, the leader of Uganda in the 1970s, expelled all the Asians living in his country. He wanted the wealth many of them had gained from their businesses to be in African hands.

APARTHEID: A NATIONAL SYSTEM OF DISCRIMINATION

The population of South Africa is about 25 million. Of these, about 5 million are white. For more than 40 years, extreme segregation of the races was enforced by laws of **apartheid** or "separate development." Only very recently, under pressure from inside and outside the country, has the white South African government declared an end to apartheid. Why was it introduced in the first place?

Two European nations led the conquest of South Africa. The Dutch arrived first, but the British took over the colony at the beginning of the nineteenth century. The descendants of the Dutch settlers, known as Afrikaners, resented British rule. Years of conflict between the two nationalities came to a climax in 1899 when war broke out. The Afrikaners were defeated and left with feelings of bitterness and hatred.

The Afrikaners believed it was their destiny to rule South Africa, a destiny given them by God. Defeat in war did not make them forget these hopes. It made them more determined to achieve their destiny. The Afrikaner Nationalist Party was elected to power in 1948. By this time, the Afrikaners no longer saw the whites of British descent as the main opposition. The black Africans were now feared as the greatest threat. To fulfill their

Under apartheid laws, black Africans had to carry a pass book. This stated which areas they were allowed to live and work in. Many Africans burned their pass books in protest.

destiny, the Afrikaners created the apartheid system, based on total white power. Opponents of apartheid were imprisoned, tortured, and murdered by the police. Nelson Mandela, the most famous black political prisoner, said at his trial in 1961, "The white man makes all the laws, he drags us before his courts and accuses us, and he sits in judgement over us. The atmosphere of white domination lurks all around this court room. It reminds me that I am voteless because there is a Parliament in this country that is white controlled. I am without land because the white minority has taken a lion's share of my country. . . . Any thinking African in this country is driven continuously to a conflict between his conscience and the law. . . . Africans, when they make their demands powerfully enough to have some chance of success, are met with force and terror from the government."

Nelson Mandela spent the next 26 years in prison, along with other African leaders who took part in the fight for freedom and equality in South Africa.

BREAKING OUT

Men and women students study on equal terms in this science laboratory class at Cairo University in Egypt.

Over thousands of years, people have fought against discrimination, whether in uprisings, wars, or, as in more modern times, by insisting on their rights in courts of law. People have also joined revolutions, in the hope of creating a new kind of society where everyone may enjoy equal rights and freedoms.

Women have played an important part in many of these struggles. They have supported revolutionary movements and campaigned for their own rights in the new society.

> "We will not hold ourselves bound by any laws in which we have no voice or representation."
>
> *Abigail Adams (1744-1818), in a letter on women's rights to her husband, John Adams, the future president*

IN THE FRONT LINE

In 1789 the people of France rebelled against the power of the king and the rich aristocrats. The revolutionaries published a famous political statement, *The Declaration of the Rights of Man and of the Citizen*. Women published their own statement, *The Declaration of the Rights of Women*. They formed their own political clubs but the male leaders of the revolution outlawed these. The men did not approve of women claiming rights for themselves.

Women were also active in the communist revolution in Russia and in the years leading to communist victory in China in 1949. Alexandra Kollontai was one of the leaders of the Russian Communist party. She hoped that both men and women would be free and equal in the new society. At first, the revolutionary government promoted women's rights, but after Joseph Stalin came to power many ideals of the revolution were lost under his tyrannical rule. Thousands suffered and died in forced labor camps.

Many women have joined movements for independence and freedom from colonial rule. The Daughters of Liberty supported the American colonies in their war of independence from Britain in 1775. Indian women joined men in nonviolent campaigns against British rule in India during the 1920s. Women fought against the French in Algeria's struggle for independence during the 1950s.

RIGHTS AT WORK

During the nineteenth and twentieth centuries workers in many parts of the world have fought for improvements in working conditions. Women have been active here, too. Women workers in the Massachusetts cotton mills helped to organize a strike for better pay in 1912. They not only had to cope with meeting and marching in freezing weather, they also faced opposition from their husbands.

Some women spent years of hard work and effort trying to enter professions. Elizabeth Blackwell was turned down by 29 American medical schools before she was finally allowed to train as a doctor. Her male teachers and fellow students refused to take her seriously. They thought the idea of a woman at medical school was a joke. However, Elizabeth Blackwell completed her training in 1849 and became America's first woman doctor. Because of her sex, she was not able to rent a house or space to use as her office, and no hospital would give her a job. She opened a new hospital run by women and later started a women's medical school.

THE VOTE

By the end of the nineteenth century the right to vote was seen as the most important issue for women. Once women could vote, it was argued, they could influence politicians. They could also enter politics themselves. Holland gave women the vote in 1893 and New Zealand did the same in 1894. In the United States and Britain women had a long, hard struggle to gain the vote. Many men opposed votes for women. These men believed that women were too stupid and too emotional to vote sensibly. Women who campaigned for the right to vote were called **suffragettes.** They tried persuading men to change their minds but when this failed they turned to stronger methods. They held marches and demonstrations. Many suffragettes were put in prison. Some went on hunger strikes to draw attention to their cause. The prison authorities reacted with force-feeding. Feeding tubes were forced down the prisoners' throats. In some cases, their health was permanently damaged. The right to vote was finally granted to American women in 1920 and to all British women in 1928. British women over the age of 30 had been given the right to vote in 1918.

WOMEN'S LIBERATION

In the 1960s campaigns for women's rights burst into life again with the women's liberation movement. Women demanded equal pay and equal job opportunities. They campaigned against sex discrimination in schools. They also demanded more and better nurseries so that mothers

Emmeline Pankhurst was one of the leaders of the women's suffrage movement in Britain. She went to prison several times for her beliefs. She is being arrested outside Buckingham Palace in 1914.

of young children could have the chance to work or study.

This women's liberation movement started in the United States. American women protested successfully against sex discrimination. Ida Phillips, a waitress earning low wages, applied for a better paying job in a factory. She was told she could not have the job because she was the mother of young children. Her supporters helped her to fight her case in the courts. Eventually, her case reached the Supreme Court — the highest court authority in the United States. The Supreme Court decided that it was against the law for companies to refuse to give jobs to mothers unless the same rule was applied to fathers.

In 1982 American women tried hard to get an Equal Rights Amendment added to the American Constitution. This would have put an end to all laws discriminating against women throughout the country, but it was not adopted because not enough politicians supported it. However, in other parts of the world, political parties started including women's rights in their programs. The governments of some newly independent nations such as Angola (1975) and Zimbabwe (1980) declared support for women's liberation. Today, women on every continent are organizing for their rights and for a better future.

"That man over there says a woman needs to be helped into carriages and lifted over ditches and to have the best place everywhere. Nobody ever helped me into carriages or over mud puddles or gives me the best places. . . . And ain't I a woman? Look at me. Look at my arm! I have ploughed and planted and gathered into barns. . . . and ain't I a woman?"

Sojourner Truth, African-American campaigner for votes for women, 1851

LOOKING FOR JUSTICE

This Mohawk Indian, wearing a chief's headdress, is taking
part in a protest in Quebec, Canada. The Mohawks took over
a golf course they claimed was on their land.

People who have experienced discrimination because of their race or religion have resisted in different ways, depending on their circumstances. Some have been able to improve their situations by peaceful means. For others the only way to survive has been to flee or to fight it out.

A SENSE OF IDENTITY

Some people have resisted discrimination by preserving their identity, in spite of being despised by others or even persecuted. Many native peoples have refused to be **assimilated** into a strange society that has no understanding of their beliefs or way of life. Many Native Americans, for example, have chosen to stand by their beliefs, customs, and traditions. They have expressed pride in their unique culture.

> "How can you respect yourself if you don't understand who you are?"
>
> *Marie Wilson, of the Gitksan people of Canada*

At one time it was government policy in Australia to assimilate the Aboriginals. Deliberate attempts were made to suppress their languages, music, and religious ceremonies. However, the Aboriginals resisted and were able to preserve their culture. It is still alive today.

CHANGING THE LAW

Laws that enforce discrimination can be changed. You saw earlier in this book how laws were changed after women won the right to vote. African-Americans tried for many years to make segregation illegal. One of the first organizations to fight segregation in the American courts was the National Association for the Advancement of Colored People (NAACP). In 1954 years of NAACP work and effort were rewarded. The Supreme Court ruled that the segregation of schools was against the spirit and meaning of the United States Constitution. Many white people in the South, however, refused to accept the

Martin Luther King, Jr., is shown here, speaking at a huge civil rights demonstration in 1963, on the steps of the Lincoln Memorial in Washington, D.C.

Supreme Court decision. Schools still refused to admit black children. The United States government had to send the army to Little Rock, Arkansas, in 1957. Nine African-American teenagers were protected by soldiers as they walked through jeering crowds into Little Rock High School.

CIVIL RIGHTS

African-Americans had to fight a long and courageous battle before segregation finally came to an end. Some whites joined them in the **civil rights movement.** Segregated buses were **boycotted** or "invaded" by black passengers. Black students sat down in "whites only" bars and restaurants. Marches and demonstrations took place all over the South and in Washington, D.C. Years of racist violence and terror had stopped most African-Americans in the southern states from voting. Civil rights workers persuaded thousands of them to vote.

"We are here this evening to say to those who have mistreated us for so long that we are tired — tired of being segregated and humiliated — tired of being kicked about by the brutal feet of oppression."

Martin Luther King, Jr., civil rights leader (1929-1968)

Some southern whites reacted to the civil rights movement with extreme violence. Civil rights campaigners were arrested and imprisoned. Many were beaten up and seriously injured. Some were brutally murdered. Film and television cameras captured the dramatic events of these years. The courage and determination of the civil rights campaigners and the ugly racism of their opponents were seen throughout the United States and in the rest of the world. Many powerful Americans declared their support for civil rights, including two presidents, John F. Kennedy and Lyndon B. Johnson.

The methods of the American civil rights movement were copied in other parts of the world. Australians organized their own civil rights campaign against the segregation of Aboriginals. Marches and demonstrations were organized in Northern Ireland as Catholics demanded an end to religious discrimination.

VIOLENT RESISTANCE

Resistance to discrimination has often involved violence, as you saw earlier in this book. Throughout the centuries ethnic and religious groups have rebelled against abuse or persecution. Sometimes violence breaks out because a peaceful campaign for equal rights is ignored or violently put down. People's patience wears thin, and they may feel they have nothing left to lose.

This feeling of desperation was behind the big city riots that took place in the United States in the mid-1960s. African-Americans were frustrated by the slow progress of the civil rights movement. Black people were angry because they felt that the police were harassing them and making use of new arrest laws to discriminate against them.

LAND RIGHTS

During the last 20 years the native peoples of America and Australia have fought for their right to own land. Mining companies tried to force the Navajo people to leave their homeland in Arizona. The Navajo refused to go. The Dene people won the legal right to own thousands of square miles of Canada's Northwest Territories. Plans to build an oil pipeline through Dene land had to be abandoned. The Dene feared the building of the pipeline would destroy wildlife. Their hunting and gathering way of life can only survive if nature is undisturbed.

> "I have dreamed on this mountain since first I was my mother's daughter
> And you just can't take my dreams away."
>
> *Navajo song of resistance*

The peoples who live in the forests of the Amazon depend on the rain forest for their survival. Every year, thousands of acres of forest are cleared to make space for farming. Many people all over the world are now campaigning to save the rain forest. They believe that if it is destroyed, the earth's climate will change. The struggle of the native peoples of the Amazon to save their environment may play an important part in protecting the future of the earth itself.

SUCCESS

Although many kinds of discrimination still continue in the world today, resistance can bring about change. The laws of the United States were changed through the efforts of the civil rights movement. Segregation was finally outlawed. The Voting Rights Act of 1965 gave African-Americans more political power than ever before.

In 1991 the South African government was forced to abandon apartheid after 40 years. In all these years Africans never gave up the struggle for freedom, and their courage inspired many people throughout the world to support them.

In 1992 the government of Brazil granted 3,628 square miles of Amazon rain forest to the Yanomani people. This was an important victory for them and their supporters abroad.

> "We are aware that the white man is sitting at our table. We know he has no right to be there; we want to remove him from our table, strip the table of all the trappings put on it by him, decorate it in true African style, settle down and then ask him to join us if he wishes."
>
> *Steve Biko, black South African political leader,*
> *murdered by the police in 1977*

The success of resistance to discrimination often depends on large numbers of people getting involved. Injustice will not go away if most people do nothing about it. If we want to see discrimination end then there are things we can do. We can support resistance movements and encourage others to do the same. We can also examine our own thoughts and feelings about people who are different from ourselves. When we meet or read about people of a different sex, race, or religion, or people who are elderly or disabled, we can listen carefully to what they say. We can try to understand and imagine what it feels like to be them. Then, perhaps, we can learn to see each other as equals.

KEY DATES

A.D. 380
Laws to discriminate: Christianity becomes the official religion of the Roman Empire and laws are passed banning Jews from positions of power.

1209
Religious persecution: Pope Innocent III announces a crusade against the Cathars.

1492
Conquest and empire: European explorers reach the Americas and claim land. Inhabitants are abused, killed, or forced into slavery for the newcomers.

1510
From freedom to slavery: Beginning of the transatlantic slave trade. Forced transportation of 12 million Africans to a life of slavery in the Americas and to centuries of oppression and prejudice.

1529
Religious wars begin in Europe: Catholic and Protestant rulers persecute and discriminate against citizens with the "wrong" beliefs for the next 200 years.

1789
Fighting for change: Revolution in France. Women claim equal rights with men as they join the struggle of the poor against the rich.

1850s
Scramble for Africa: European countries, led by Britain and France, claim large parts of Africa for themselves. Whole societies are placed under colonial rule that heavily discriminates against them.

1865
Freedom or fear? End of slavery in the United States. African-Americans are granted citizenship and given the right to vote. In the South white racists start taking these rights away.

1920
Finding a voice: Women in the United States gain the right to vote after a long campaign by suffragettes.

1933
Minorities destroyed: The Nazis seize power in Germany. Discrimination against Jews and gypsies is introduced and finally leads to mass murder of millions.

1948
Divide and discriminate: The Afrikaner Nationalist Party gains power in South Africa and begins to introduce apartheid.

1955
Power of protest: African-Americans in Montgomery, Alabama, boycott city buses. This marks the start of a ten-year campaign for equal rights.

1964
Outlawed: Discrimination on grounds of race, color, religion, sex, or national origin is made illegal in the United States. Eleven years later race discrimination is made illegal in Australia; race and sex discrimination outlawed in Britain by 1976.

1991
A fresh start? The government of South Africa announces the end of apartheid.

GLOSSARY

apartheid: Keeping races of a country separate from each other by force or law.

assimilate: To become absorbed. Ethnic or religious minorities that become assimilated abandon their own traditions and ways of life and adopt those of the majority.

boycott: To refuse to buy something. Boycotts have often been used as political weapons. Opponents of apartheid in many countries have boycotted products made or grown in South Africa.

caste: A system of dividing society into unequal groups according to birth. Individuals cannot move into a different group by their own efforts. The Indian caste system was based on the Hindu religion. Marriage between people of different castes was not allowed and contact was restricted by religious rules.

civil rights movement: An American political movement of the 1950s and 1960s that aimed to end racial segregation and ensure equal rights for African-Americans.

colony: 1) A settlement of newcomers in a foreign land. 2) A land that is governed by a country overseas.

communism: A political theory based on the ideas of Karl Marx (1818-1883). Communists believe in a social and economic system where wealth and property are owned jointly by all citizens. In the world's main communist countries (China and the former Soviet Union) wealth and property were taken over by the state and political power was kept

firmly in the hands of the Communist parties themselves.

concentration camp: First used to describe prison camps set up by the British during the South African war against the Dutch settlers (1899-1902). Stalin used concentration camps to imprison political opponents in the Soviet Union. The Nazis used them to imprison and murder political opponents, Jews, gypsies, and other minority groups.

crusade: A war to defend one particular religious faith against another. In fact such wars often had more to do with preserving power and wealth than defending the faith.

democracy: A system of government that answers to the people and that allows different political views.

discrimination: Unequal treatment of a group of people on account of race, nationality, religion, sex, or ability.

ghetto: Originally a part of a European town in the Middle Ages where Jews were allowed to live. The word is now used to mean poor, run-down parts of American cities.

immigrant: A person who comes to a foreign country to live.

industrial revolution: A period in European history, from about 1760 to about 1880, when industry was introduced and developed on a large scale. Many people left the land to work in the new factories and live in towns.

minority: A distinct group of people within the total population of a country.

Nazi: National Socialist Party, a German political party led by Adolf Hitler. The Nazis believed in the superiority of the white race and they preached racial hatred, particularly hatred of the Jews. They ruled Germany from 1933 to 1945.

pagan: Ancient religious beliefs existing before Christianity. Many pagan religions include the worship of nature or gods and goddesses of nature.

persecution: Harsh and obvious discrimination, usually involving force and violence.

privilege: Benefits or advantages that some people have and others do not, such as inherited wealth.

racism: Prejudice against and hatred of people based on their race. Racism involves beliefs about some races being superior to others.

segregation: Keeping people separate along lines of race, sex, or religion.

social class: A system dividing societies into unequal groups based on differences in wealth, jobs, and education.

socialism: A political belief that stresses equality of wealth. Socialists believe that society should not be sharply divided into rich and poor and that land and businesses should not be owned by individuals but by the community as a whole.

suffragettes: British and American women who campaigned for the vote. The word suffrage means the right to vote.

INDEX